BAR GRAPHS

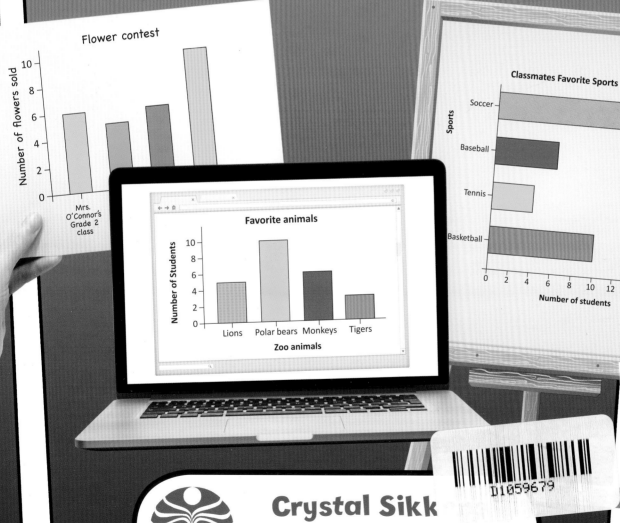

Flower contest

Number of flowers sold

Mrs. O'Connor's Grade 2 class

Favorite animals

Number of Students

Lions Polar bears Monkeys Tigers

Zoo animals

Classmates Favorite Sports

Sports

Soccer

Baseball

Tennis

Basketball

Number of students

Crystal Sikk

Crabtree Publishing Company

www.crabtreebooks.com

GET GRAPHING!
Building Data Literacy Skills

Author: Crystal Sikkens

Series research and development:
Reagan Miller

Editorial director: Kathy Middleton

Photo research: Crystal Sikkens,
Katherine Berti

Design: Katherine Berti

Proofreader: Janine Deschenes

Indexer: Petrice Custance

Print and production coordinator:
Katherine Berti

Image credits:
Shutterstock: © Anton_Ivanov p 21 (bottom left);
© Irina Silvestrova p 21 (bottom center)
All other images by Shutterstock

Library and Archives Canada Cataloguing in Publication

Sikkens, Crystal, author
        Bar graphs / Crystal Sikkens.

(Get graphing! Building data literacy skills)
Includes index.
Issued in print and electronic formats.
ISBN 978-0-7787-2624-1 (hardback).--
ISBN 978-0-7787-2634-0 (paperback).--
ISBN 978-1-4271-1837-0 (html)

        1. Graphic methods--Juvenile literature. 2. Charts, diagrams,
etc.--Juvenile literature. 3. Mathematics--Charts, diagrams, etc.--Juvenile
literature. I. Title.

QA90.S545 2016   j518'.23   C2016-903315-5
                                          C2016-903316-3

Library of Congress Cataloging-in-Publication Data

CIP available at the Library of Congress

Crabtree Publishing Company
www.crabtreebooks.com   1-800-387-7650

Printed in Canada/072016/EF20160630

Published in Canada
Crabtree Publishing
616 Welland Ave.
St. Catharines, Ontario
L2M 5V6

Published in the United States
Crabtree Publishing
PMB 59051
350 Fifth Avenue, 59th Floor
New York, New York 10118

Published in the United Kingdom
Crabtree Publishing
Maritime House
Basin Road North, Hove
BN41 1WR

Published in Australia
Crabtree Publishing
3 Charles Street
Coburg North
VIC 3058

Contents

Sharing Information   4

Different Graphs   6

Bar Graph Parts   8

Same and Different   10

Collecting Data   12

Creating a Bar Graph   14

Adding the Data   16

The Final Results   18

Choosing a Trip   20

Favorite Animals   22

Learning More and
   About the Author   23

Glossary, Index,
   and Answers   24

Sharing Information

Information, or **data**, is all around us. We can find it in books, newspapers, on television, and on the Internet. People **communicate**, or share data with others through photographs, words, and drawings.

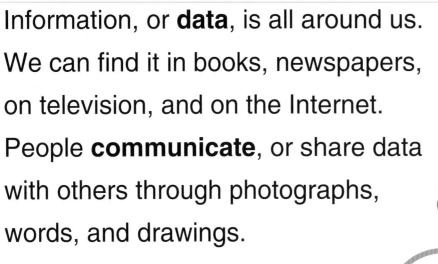

A lot of data can be found in the books and computers in your school library.

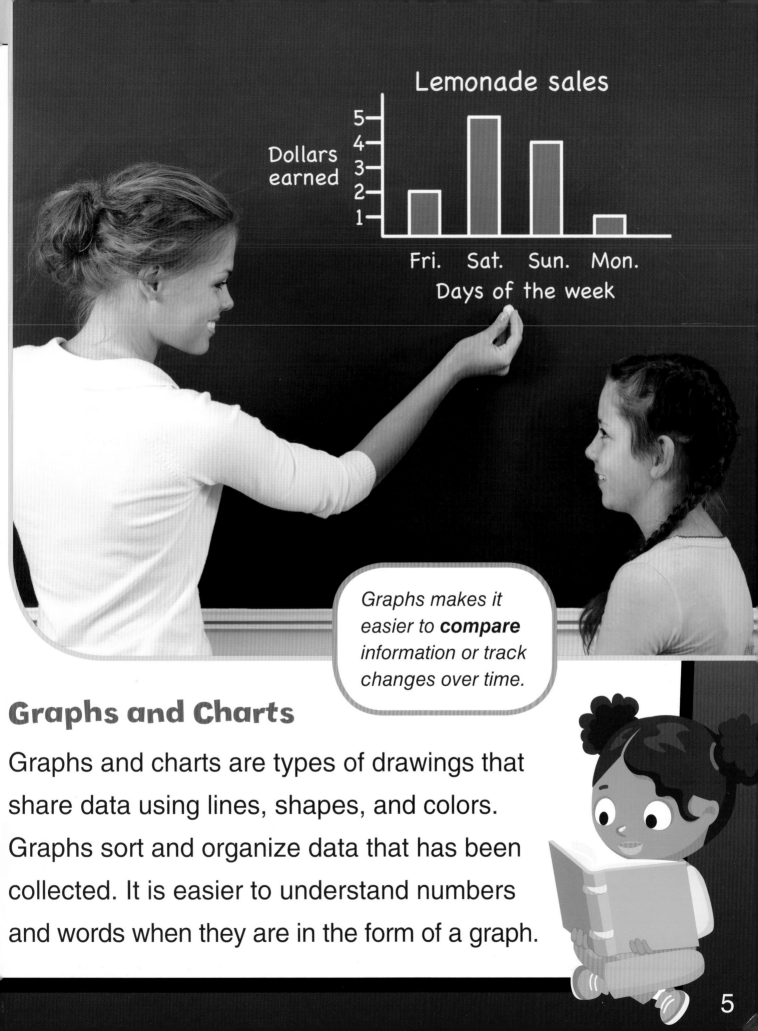

Lemonade sales

Dollars earned

5
4
3
2
1

Fri.   Sat.   Sun.   Mon.

Days of the week

Graphs makes it easier to **compare** information or track changes over time.

Graphs and Charts

Graphs and charts are types of drawings that share data using lines, shapes, and colors. Graphs sort and organize data that has been collected. It is easier to understand numbers and words when they are in the form of a graph.

Different Graphs

There are many different kinds of graphs. Bar graphs, line graphs, and picture graphs are the most common kinds. Each kind of graph is used to show different kinds of information.

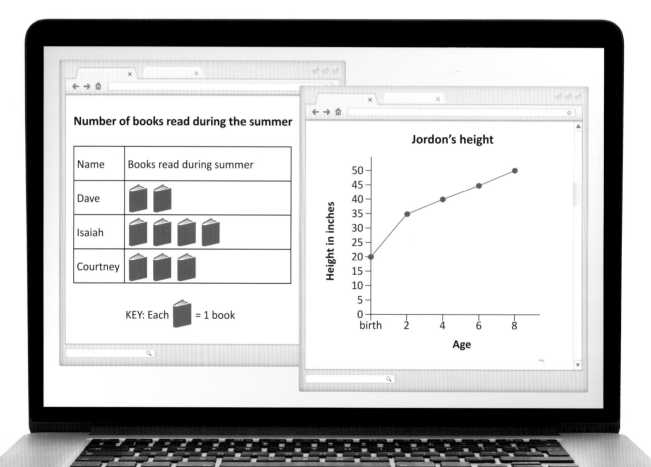

Number of books read during the summer

Name	Books read during summer
Dave	📚📚
Isaiah	📚📚📚📚
Courtney	📚📚📚

KEY: Each 📕 = 1 book

Jordon's height

A picture graph is a graph that uses pictures to compare information.

Line graphs use points and lines to show small changes over a period of time.

Bar Graphs

In this book, you will learn all about bar graphs. Bar graphs compare information like a picture graph, but instead of using pictures, bar graphs show the information using colored bars of different lengths.

Be a Data Detective!

1. *Which type of graph would you use if you wanted to show temperature changes in a day?*

2. *Which would you use if you wanted to compare the height of three different plants?*

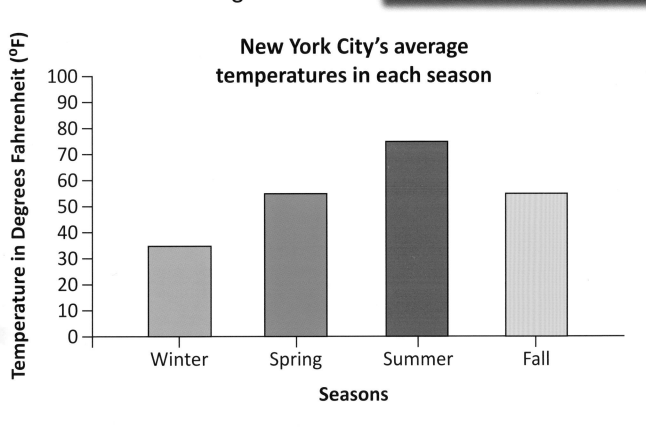

New York City's average temperatures in each season

Temperature in Degrees Fahrenheit (°F)

100
90
80
70
60
50
40
30
20
10
0

Winter   Spring   Summer   Fall

Seasons

Bar graphs can also be used to show larger changes over time.

Bar Graph Parts

All bar graphs include the same main parts. Each part has a different job that helps you read and understand the graph. Knowing the different parts will help you create your own bar graphs.

*The **scale** is the range of numbers that is marked on an axis.*

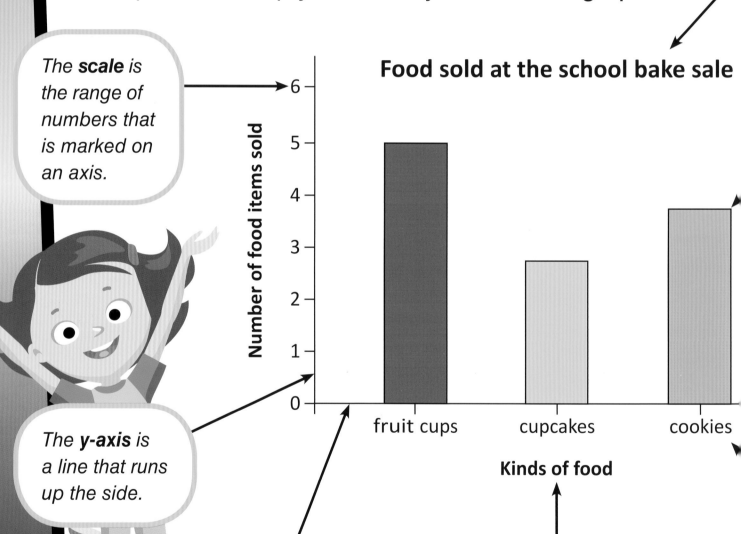

Food sold at the school bake sale

Number of food items sold

Kinds of food

fruit cups   cupcakes   cookies

*The **y-axis** is a line that runs up the side.*

*The **x-axis** is a line that runs along the bottom of the graph.*

*The axis **labels** give information about the facts shown on the graph, such as the number and type of data being compared.*

The **title** of a bar graph tells readers what information is being shown on the graph.

The **bars** show the data. Longer bars represent larger numbers.

Why are the categories an important part of a bar graph?

muffins

The **categories** show what each bar represents.

9

Same and Different

The same data can be shown in two different ways on a bar graph. The data can be displayed on a **vertical** bar graph or a **horizontal** bar graph. On a vertical bar graph, the bars go up and down. Horizontal bar graphs have the bars going from side to side.

Vertical bar graph

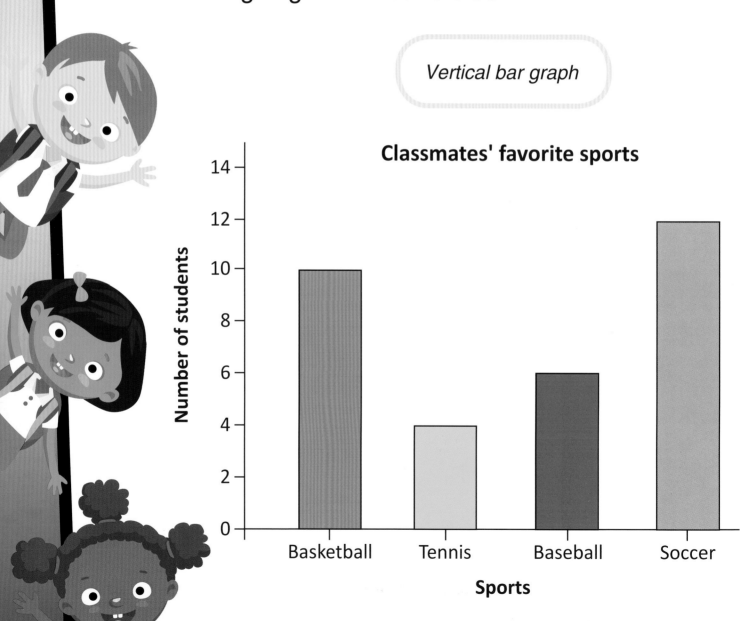

Classmates' favorite sports

Horizontal and Vertical

On a vertical bar graph, the categories, or things being compared, are listed on the x-axis. The y-axis contains the scale. On a horizontal bar graph, the y-axis contains the categories and the x-axis has the scale. Horizontal bar graphs are often used when the categories have long labels.

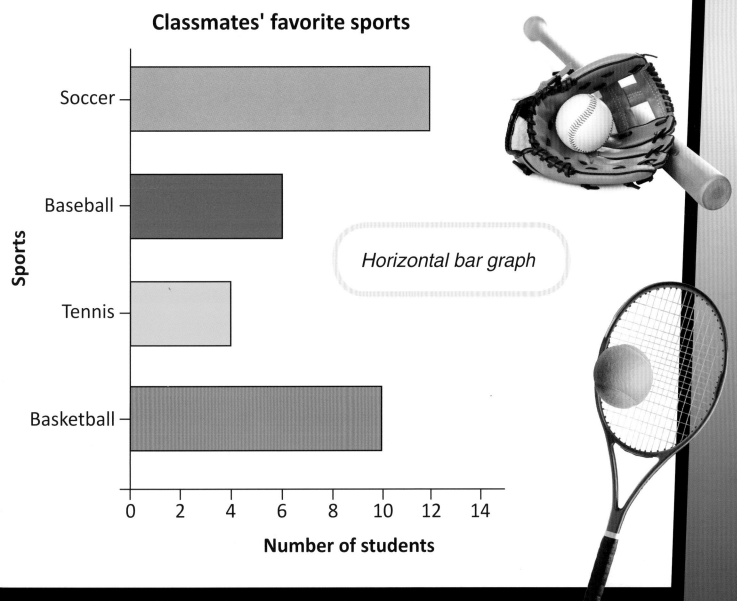

Classmates' favorite sports

Horizontal bar graph

Collecting Data

Mia Williams is a grade 2 student. Her teacher, Mrs. O'Connor, told her class that for the next two weeks the school's grade 2 and 3 classes will be selling flowers to raise money for new computers in the library. The class that sells the most flowers gets to go on a field trip of their choice at the end of the year.

Tally Charts

Mia really wants to win the contest, because she loves going on field trips. After the first week, Mia wanted to see whether her class was ahead. She found out how many flowers each class has sold so far and marked them on a **tally chart** using **tally marks**.

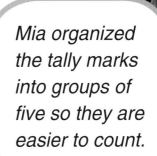

Number of flowers sold

Mrs. O'Connor's Grade 2 class	|||||	
Mr. Dekker's Grade 2 class	|||||
Mrs. Fung's Grade 3 class	|||||	
Mr. Bauer's Grade 3 class	||||| |||||

Mia organized the tally marks into groups of five so they are easier to count.

Creating a Bar Graph

Mia wanted to share the data she collected with the rest of the class. She decided the easiest way to show her data and compare the **results** was to create a graph. She decided to draw a vertical bar graph. She began by adding a title and drawing a line for the x-axis and a line for the y-axis.

Mia added labels on the x-axis and y-axis. She also added categories listing the grade 2 and 3 classes on the x-axis.

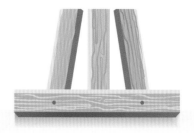

Flower contest

Number of flowers sold

| Mrs. Connor's Grade 2 class | Mr. Dekker's Grade 2 class | Mrs. Fung's Grade 3 class | Mrs. Bauer's Grade 3 class |

Classes

Scale

Mia now needed to determine the scale for the y-axis. To determine the scale, Mia looked at the largest and smallest numbers on her tally chart. Ten was the largest and six was the smallest. She decided a scale where the numbers went up by 2 would make the graph the easiest to read. She started the scale at 0. Each number she added to the axis was two more than the one below it.

Mia added marks to the y-axis that were about the same distance apart.

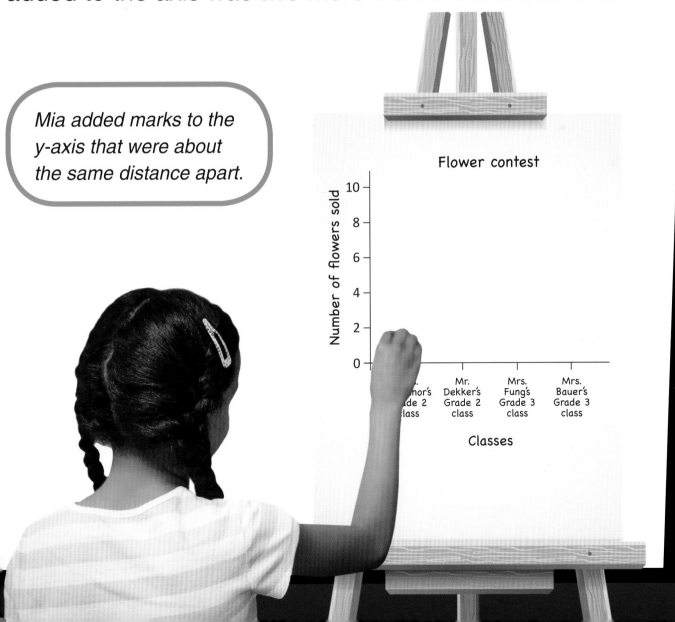

Flower contest

Number of flowers sold

Classes

Adding the Data

Next, Mia added the data to her graph. Mia drew a bar in the shape of a rectangle for each of the four classes on her tally chart. The top of each bar lined up with the number on the scale that matched the amount of flowers that each class sold.

Be a Data Detective!

1. *Using Mia's graph, which class has sold the most flowers so far?*

2. *Is Mia's class winning?*

Mr. Dekker's class sold 5 flowers. Mia put the top of that bar between the 4 and 6 marks on the scale.

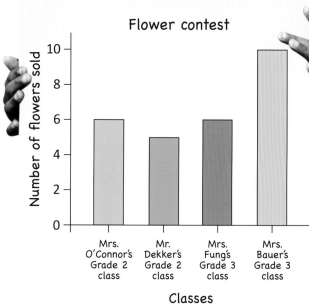

Flower contest

Number of flowers sold

Classes

Mrs. O'Connor's Grade 2 class — Mr. Dekker's Grade 2 class — Mrs. Fung's Grade 3 class — Mrs. Bauer's Grade 3 class

Colored Bars

Sometimes the bars on bar graphs are different colors to make the data easier to read. The same colors can be used to show data with the same amounts, or to highlight certain groups or features.

Be a Data Detective!

Which graph below makes it easier to find the total amount of flowers the Grade 2 classes sold?

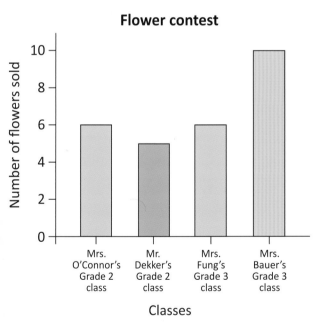

In this graph, the bars for Mrs. O'Connor's class and Mrs. Fung's class are the same color because they both sold 6 flowers.

In this graph, the same color bars are used to highlight the Grade 2 and Grade 3 classes.

Based on Mia's graph, her class knew they were tied for second place after the first week of flower sales. This data showed them that they needed to try and sell more flowers in the second week in order to win. After the two weeks were over, Mrs. O'Connor gave the class the tally chart below with the final results.

Number of flowers sold

Mrs. O'Connor's Grade 2 class	ⵑ ⵑ ⵑ ⵑ ⵑ ⵑ ⵑ |
Mr. Dekker's Grade 2 class	ⵑ ⵑ ⵑ ⵑ | |
Mrs. Fung's Grade 3 class	ⵑ ⵑ | | | |
Mr. Bauer's Grade 3 class	ⵑ ⵑ ⵑ ⵑ | | | |

Be a Data Detective!

1. Which bar graph shows the correct results from the tally chart on page 18?

2. Did Mrs. O'Connor's class win the contest?

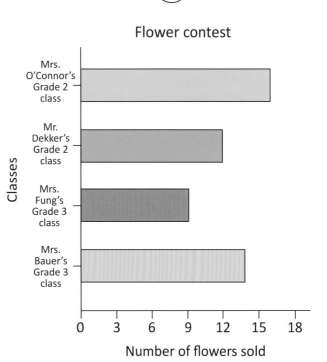

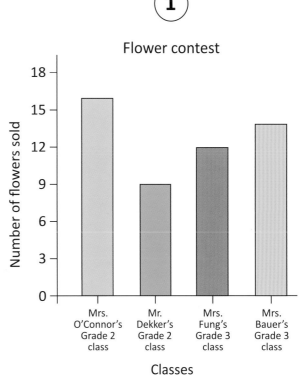

Flower contest

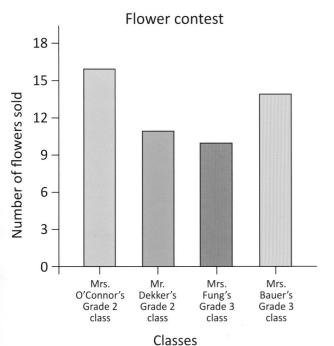

Choosing a Trip

Mia and her classmates are happy to find out they won the contest! Now they get to choose a place to go on their field trip. Mrs. O'Connor gives the class four places to choose from. She takes a **survey** of the class to find out where everyone wants to go. The place with the most votes is where the class will go on their trip.

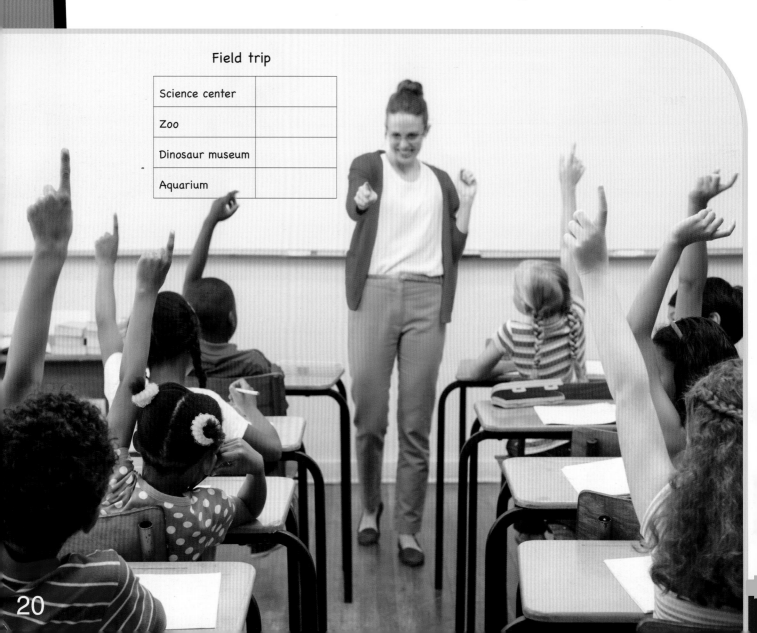

Field trip

Science center	
Zoo	
Dinosaur museum	
Aquarium	

Now It's Your Turn!

Create your own bar graph using the results from Mrs. O'Connor's survey found in the tally chart below.

Field trip

Science center	||||
Zoo	|||| |||| ||
Dinosaur museum	|||| |||
Aquarium	|||

Remember to make sure you have all the parts on your graph:

✔ title
✔ y-axis
✔ x-axis
✔ labels
✔ categories
✔ scale
✔ bars

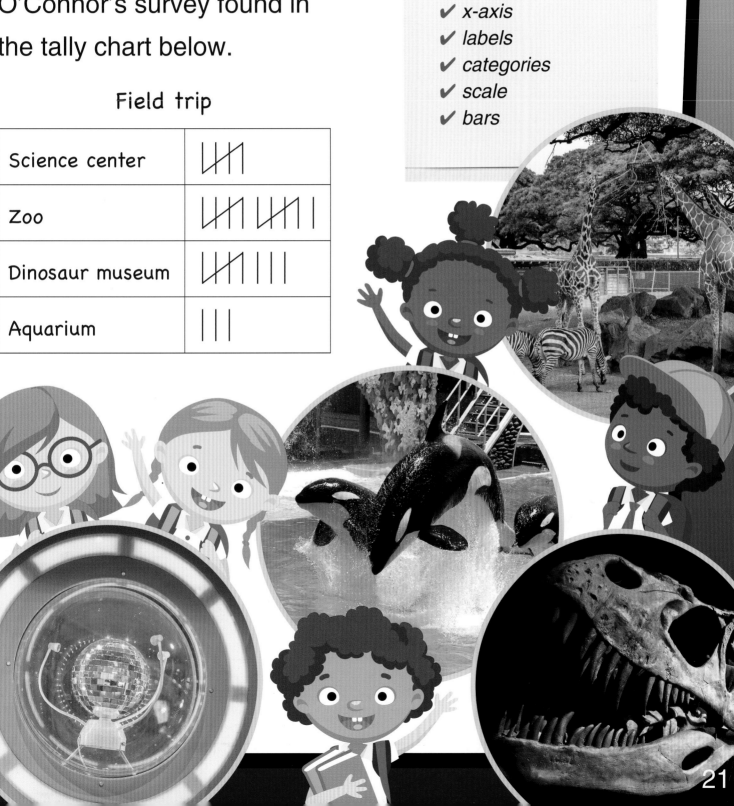

21

Favorite Animals

After they got back from their zoo field trip, Mia took a survey of the class to find out which animals they liked best. She put the results in the graph below. By reading the graph, it is easy to see that most students liked the polar bears best.

Be a Data Detective!

Use Mia's graph to answer the questions below.

1. What is the difference between the number of votes for the polar bears and for the tigers?

2. How many students voted on Mia's survey in total?

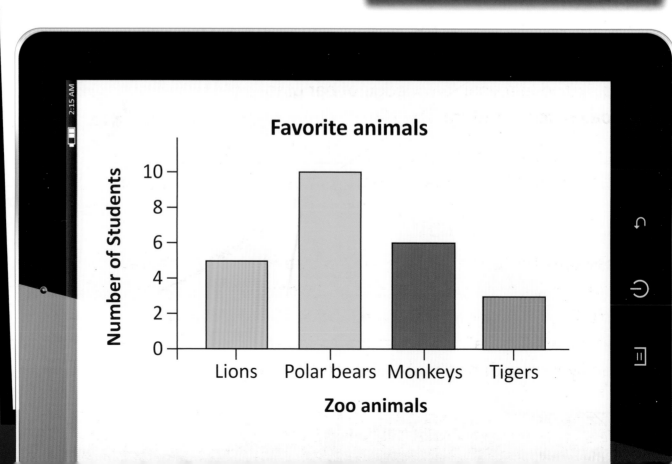